ADD AND ADHD

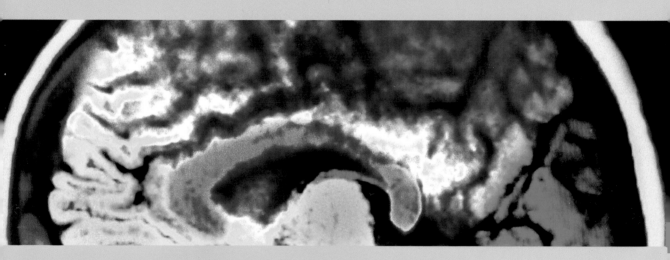

George Capaccio

Marshall Cavendish
Benchmark
New York

Marshall Cavendish Benchmark
99 White Plains Road
Tarrytown, New York 10591-9001
www.marshallcavendish.us

This book is not intended for use as a substitute for advice, consultation, or treatment by a licensed medical practitioner. The reader is advised that no action of a medical nature should be taken without consultation with a licensed medical practitioner, including action that may seem to be indicated by the contents of this work, since individual circumstances vary and medical standards, knowledge, and practices change with time. The publisher, author, and medical consultants disclaim all liability and cannot be held responsible for any problems that may arise from use of this book.

Library of Congress Cataloging-in-Publication Data

Capaccio, George.
  ADD and ADHD / by George Capaccio.
      p. cm. — (Health alert)
  Summary: "Discusses ADD and ADHD and their effects on people and society"—Provided by publisher.
  Includes bibliographical references and index.
  ISBN 978-0-7614-2705-6
  1. Attention-deficit hyperactivity disorder—Juvenile literature. I. Title. II. Series.

  RJ506.H9C362 2008
  616.85'89—dc22

                                        2007008790

Front cover: Ritalin pills
Title page: A scan of the human brain

Photo research by Candlepants, Inc.
Front cover: © Richard T. Nowitz/PhotoTakeUSA.com
The photographs in this book are used by permission and through the courtesy of:
Photo Researchers Inc.: Scott Camazine & Sue Trainor, 1, 24; Andrew Paul Leonard, 3, 22; James Cavallini, 21; Phanie, 33; Charles Bach, 44; Voisin, 49; LADA, 55. *Getty Images:* Time Life Pictures, 9; Time Life Pictures, 13. *Corbis:* Grace/zefa, 10, 16. *The Image Works:* Ellen B. Senisi, 17, 19, 46, 47, 51, 54, 57; John Griffin, 27, 48. *PhotoTakeUSA.com:* John W. Karapelou, CMI, 23; © Richard T. Nowitz, 39. *Index Stock:* Ewing Galloway, 34. *AP Images:* Chuck Burton, 37. *Custom Medical Stock Photo:* 40.

Printed in China
6 5 4 3 2

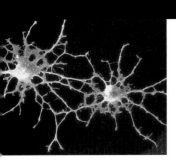

CONTENTS

WHAT IS IT LIKE TO HAVE ADD OR ADHD?

PENNY'S STORY

When Penny was very young, she enjoyed making up bedtime stories with her mother. They called them Faraway Stories because they were about children who lived in Faraway Land, a magical place far from the cares of the day. Penny was more like her mother than her four brothers or even her father. She was quiet and shy, and liked to spend a lot of time alone. But she often had trouble remembering the right word when she wanted to ask about something. So she would make up a new word or phrase. "That plane place" was Penny's phrase for airport. "Box-day thing" was how she described someone's birthday.

Penny did not start forming simple sentences until she was three years old. Her parents worried that there might be something wrong with Penny since her ability to express herself was behind other children her age. They took her to see a doctor who recommended that Penny's mother spend time each day reading to her daughter and creating stories with her. The doctor hoped that these activities might improve Penny's language skills. That is how the Faraway Stories got started. The stories helped bring mother and daughter closer together but they did not solve the problems Penny was beginning to have at school.

As far back as first grade, Penny had trouble paying attention. Her mind seemed to be somewhere else, and she constantly had to be reminded to do her schoolwork. Even though she loved books, she had trouble understanding what she read. Year after year, she fell further behind in reading. When Penny was in the fifth grade, her teacher recommended that her parents bring her to see a **psychiatrist.** The teacher had some experience dealing with children like Penny and suspected Penny's difficulties in school might be caused by an attention disorder.

The psychiatrist wanted to talk with Penny's parents before meeting Penny. The doctor asked them many questions about Penny's life to help him make a diagnosis. Then, instead of interviewing Penny in his office, he decided to observe her in her classroom. The doctor felt this would give him a much clearer understanding of her behavior. With the teacher's permission, he sat in on Penny's math period. One of the first things he noticed was that Penny's chair was in the back of the room and right beside the windows. During a lesson about fractions, Penny spent most of the time looking out the window. Whenever she looked at the blackboard, she seemed lost, as though she did not understand what the teacher was talking about.

After class, the psychiatrist spoke in private with Penny. Penny told him that during the math lesson, she had made up a story about people who looked like numbers. She had imagined squat old men who looked like sixes and funny old women who resembled nines. The men and women began to dance with one another, and as they did, Penny said, they turned into eights.

Penny also told the psychiatrist that she got along well with the other children in her class and really liked her teachers. But she felt bad about always being behind in her schoolwork. The psychiatrist talked with Penny's teacher and also interviewed her parents one more time. When he felt he had enough information, he concluded that Penny had Attention Deficit Disorder (ADD). (The newest medical guidelines call Penny's problem Attention Deficit Hyperactivity Disorder (ADHD) without **hyperactivity.**) He prescribed a drug called Norpramin, which is used in treating this disorder.

Penny took the medication once a day, and within a few days, her teacher and her parents noticed a dramatic difference in her behavior. At school, she was able to pay closer attention during lessons. She also seemed to enjoy learning and became much more outgoing with her classmates. But the medication did not dampen Penny's wonderful imagination. Seeing the positive changes in her daughter, her mother said, "It's as if a veil has been lifted from Penny's eyes. She can see us and we can see her. She's still my dreamer, but now she can focus, too."

DONALD'S STORY

As a child, Donald could not sit still long enough to watch a television program or listen to his mother read to him. For most of his waking hours, he was on the go, getting into things, and racing from one toy or playtime activity to another. He had a very short attention span, and was easily frustrated when things did not go his way. Donald found it difficult to make friends with children his own age.

Even though Donald was smart, he did not do well at school, and was three years behind in reading, spelling, and math. He often forgot to bring his school books home with him and rarely completed his homework assignments. In middle school, Donald began stealing other people's things. Eventually, he got caught and got into trouble. Donald's mother and teachers decided that he should speak with a **therapist** at a child guidance clinic.

The therapist was a psychiatrist like Penny's doctor. After interviewing Donald and his parents, he determined that Donald had ADHD. He put Donald on a drug called **Ritalin.** Donald responded well to his medication. The dosage, or amount, of Ritalin was gradually increased as they monitored how Donald was doing.

At school, Donald's grades improved as he became more focused and more able to tolerate frustration. He also got along better with his classmates and began having more friends his own age. Donald stopped stealing and getting into trouble.

Penny and Donald are among millions of school-age children who have ADHD. Because of these conditions, they behave in ways that cause serious problems for themselves and their families. These children often have trouble concentrating, exercising self-control, and do not consider the consequences, or the possible results, of their actions. They may have normal intelligence or may even be gifted. But the difficulties they have with staying focused can have a very negative effect on how they relate to others—including family members—and how well they do at school. Fortunately, there are medications and forms of treatment that can help many of these children. With this help, they can be as happy, healthy, and productive as other children their age.

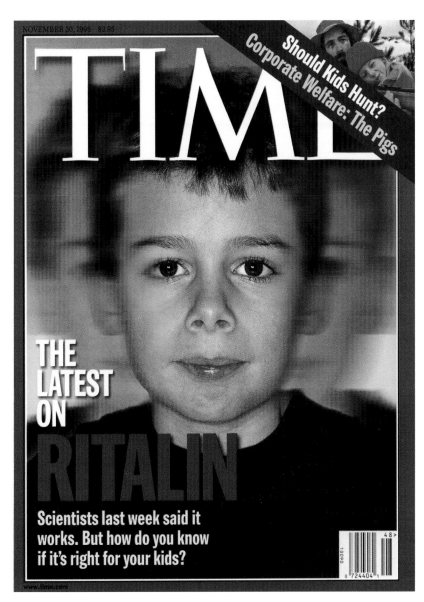

Though attention disorders have been around for thousands of years, ADHD and its treatments have been in the news more frequently over the past several years.

2

WHAT ARE ADD AND ADHD?

Attention Deficit Hyperactivity Disorder is not a learning disability. It has nothing to do with low intelligence or mental disability, and it is not related to problems with acquiring language skills. Current research indicates that ADHD is more likely the result of brain chemistry. People whose brains do not have enough of certain chemicals may develop ADHD. External factors, like how parents raise their child, may help or worsen this condition. But the condition itself, in most cases, is based on a child's unique biology. This means that the condition

Most children with attention disorders, such as ADD or ADHD, have trouble focusing on tasks like doing their homework.

occurs because of the way the child's brain is organized or wired.

SYMPTOMS

ADHD can occur in boys or girls, and in men or women. It can affect rich people as well poor people, and can be found in all ethnic groups throughout society. But it is not always easy to determine who has these conditions. One of the symptoms, or signs of ADHD is hyperactivity. Hyperactive children are full of energy and always on the go. For example, they often cannot sit still long enough to read a book or complete a homework assignment. But most children, when they are young, love to be active, to explore the world around them instead of staying in one place. Does this mean they have ADHD? Not necessarily—it may only mean that they are just behaving like children.

ADD or ADHD?

In the past, people who had attention deficit disorders but no hyperactivity were diagnosed with ADD. However, health professionals now feel that ADD is a form of ADHD, without the hyperactivity. So when they diagnose a child with an attention disorder they now call it ADHD and not ADD. In this book, you will see that ADHD is used to refer to all attention deficit disorders—which would include the disorder that was once called ADD.

The same holds true for other symptoms associated with ADHD, such as poor concentration and weak self-control. It takes time for a child to learn how to concentrate, or stay on task. Children must also learn how to control their impulses and think about the consequences of their actions. Learning these things is simply part of growing up. But from the time they are very young, children with ADHD behave in ways that set them part. Their difficulties with paying attention or sitting quietly are much more severe and last far longer. ADHD is often referred to as a syndrome, which is any group of related symptoms. So what are the main symptoms of ADHD?

Hyperactivity

Hyperactivity is certainly one of them. But not all children diagnosed with ADHD are hyperactive. In school, children with ADHD but no hyperactivity daydream a lot and often fall behind in their lessons. Many of these children are withdrawn and passive, which means they do not spend a lot of time interacting with their teachers or classmates.

Boys who are hyperactive tend to move about frequently. In school, they may find it hard to stay in their seats or to keep from talking out loud. Hyperactive girls, on the other hand, are more likely to engage in less noticeable behaviors like fidgeting in their seats, whispering to their neighbors, or doodling a lot in their notebooks.

Boys and girls with ADHD have a hard time sitting still, and often feel the need to move around from place to place.

Hyperactivity usually begins when the child with ADHD is very young. This symptom expresses itself in different ways as the child grows. Hyperactive infants are likely to be very squirmy and to have trouble falling and staying asleep. As toddlers, these children often get into everything and seem to have an inexhaustible supply of energy. Hyperactive school-age children can be extremely restless during class time. Of course, part of this restlessness might be a response to lessons that are

Boys and Girls

....

Studies have shown that boys in elementary school are more likely than girls to be **diagnosed** with ADHD. This is mainly because boys show their hyperactivity in obvious ways. Girls, on the other hand, express their hyperactivity in less obvious ways. Because symptoms in girls with ADHD are less likely to be noticed, these girls are also less likely to be diagnosed with the disorder.

One of the first scientific studies of girls with ADHD was conducted in 2003. But scientists have been researching boys with ADHD for about 100 years. Today, researchers estimate that about 75 percent of girls with ADHD are not diagnosed in elementary school. They may not be diagnosed until they are in middle school, high school, or even college.

dull and repetitious. But unlike children who do not have ADHD, the hyperactive child has a great deal of trouble focusing. In class, whether the lesson is interesting or not, he or she just cannot seem to slow down long enough to pay attention and do the work.

The flip side of hyperactivity is **hyperfocus.** Some hyperactive children can become so absorbed in a task or activity, like drawing, that they lose all track of time. They may even become unaware of what is going on around them. Usually, these children are very interested in whatever activity has their attention. But scientists still do not understand why some hyperactive children are able to hyperfocus. Could these same children choose to concentrate on a subject that does not interest them? In other words, could they force themselves to focus?

Research suggests that for hyperactive children, will power is not enough. No matter how hard they try, they just cannot slow down long enough—unless they find the subject very interesting. But that is no guarantee that they will be able to concentrate for a length of time.

Short Attention Spans

Having a short attention span is another important symptom of ADHD. (In fact, the word *deficit* means there is not enough of something. In this case, there is not enough attention.) For example, a preschooler or kindergartener with ADHD may go through many toys or playtime activities in a short period of time. Nothing seems to hold his or her attention for very long. He may scatter crayons over the desk, flip rapidly through the pages of a storybook, or not remember the instructions the teacher has given. A child like this is easily distracted—by his or her own thoughts and by whatever is going on outside or inside the classroom.

At home, a child with ADHD may forget to clean up his or her room after making a mess. He or she may also have trouble getting ready for school. Deciding which clothes to wear can be a frustrating task for a child with ADHD. In extreme cases, parents may need to write out clear instructions for the children to follow. Such instructions guide the children as they prepare for school or clean their rooms. The childrens' difficulty

Daydreaming is common in all children. But children with ADHD daydream more than others because they have difficulty concentrating.

at home or in school has nothing to do with their level of intelligence. Instead, it is a sign of how the brain is handling information, or data, coming from the outside world.

Impulse Control

Children with ADHD are likely to have poor control over their impulses. This means that when they want to do something, they do it. Often, they do not plan ahead or consider the consequences. Such **impulsivity** can lead to injury or even land the ADHD child in a lot of trouble. There is an old saying that cautions people to "look before you leap." In other words, think before you act. Unfortunately, children with ADHD act first. Like other children, they may be tempted to play with things that are off limits, or may think about stealing from others. But as they get older, children with ADHD who continue to have poor impulse control can get into serious trouble.

Educational Development

Children with ADHD are likely to experience difficulties in school no matter how intelligent they are. Because their overall mental abilities tend to develop unevenly, they might do really well in math but do poorly in reading or spelling. Also, problems with poor concentration and a short attention span make learning even more challenging. This is especially true for children with ADHD who consistently get low grades on papers and tests. If their teachers and parents criticize them for failing or falling

This young student with ADHD is in a special math class with teachers that help him focus on the work and complete it at his own pace.

behind, they will often develop low **self-esteem** and will lack confidence in their abilities. As a result, they will not be motivated to try harder and will fall even further behind. In teenagers with ADHD, these problems in school, lack of motivation, and low self-esteem may lead to dropping out of school completely.

Emotional Development

Emotional problems are another characteristic of many children with ADHD. Besides having low self-esteem, they might not be able to tolerate too much frustration or disappointment. At times when they do not get their own way, they may overreact by having a temper tantrum or becoming withdrawn and ignoring everything. Children with ADHD also tend to be more excitable than other children. In certain situations, they can become over-stimulated and may not be able to control their reactions. For instance, a trip to the supermarket where there are so many things to look at and touch may be too much to handle. He or she may throw a tantrum or burst into tears from all the activity.

Generally speaking, children with ADHD tend to behave like children several years younger than them. Compared to their peers, they are immature. For example, a ten-year-old child with ADHD often acts like a normal four- or five-year old. That is, he does not follow directions very well, has poor social

Children with poor impulse control often throw tantrums and act out in frustration.

skills, may lack physical coordination, and will find it hard to stick to one thing for very long.

CAUSES OF ADHD

Researchers have been studying ADHD for a very long time. They have identified at least three leading causes. Premature birth is one of them. A child who is born earlier than planned is likely to be underweight and very small. In many cases, the baby has not had enough time to develop, which can lead to health problems, including ADHD.

Lead poisoning is another cause of ADHD. At one time, paints used in the home were mixed with lead, a type of metal that can be very poisonous to humans. When children ate chips of lead paint from the walls or windowsills of their home, they risked developing ADHD. Fortunately, lead paint is no longer manufactured. But it still has not been removed from many older homes. So the danger of lead poisoning continues.

In the 1920s manufacturers began adding lead to gasoline for cars and other vehicles. The burning of leaded gas from the 1920s to the 1980s was responsible for about 90 percent of the lead in the air. During that same period, about 68 million children in the United States were exposed to fumes from leaded gas. Inhaling these fumes put them at risk for developing hyperactivity and a shortened attention span—two of the symptoms of ADHD. Fortunately, the Environmental Protection Agency (EPA) began phasing out leaded gas in the 1970s. In the 1990s, laws were passed that banned the sale and use of leaded fuel for all overland vehicles like cars, buses, and trucks. It is possible that this decrease of lead in the air has helped to lower the number of cases of ADHD.

By far, the leading cause of ADHD is genetic transmission. This means that ADHD is an inherited condition that is passed on through the parents' genes to the child. Genes determine whether a person will be tall or short, have brown eyes or blue, and other characteristics. A great deal of research still needs to be done on the role of genes in ADHD. But it appears that certain genes may control how the brain produces and uses

The chromosomes shown here are made up of genes. All of this genetic material helps to determine people's physical characteristics, as well as how their bodies and brains function.

chemicals called **neurotransmitters,** which in turn, can affect ADHD.

THE BRAIN AND ADHD

The human brain contains about 100 billion nerve cells, or **neurons.** Like a huge communications network, the brain is constantly processing messages from all parts of the body. For example, when your feet get cold in the winter, neurons relay the message of "cold" to a part of your brain. You can then

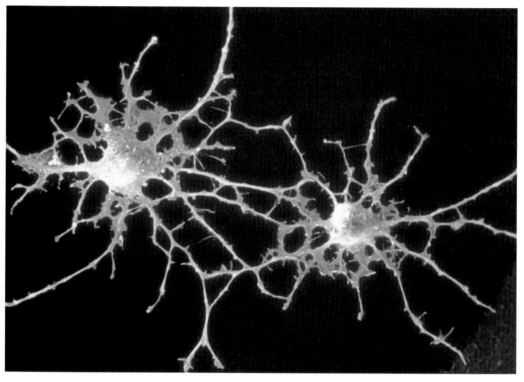

A human being has millions of nerve cells throughout the body.

choose to respond by putting on heavier socks or changing your shoes. Something similar happens when you feel hungry or sleepy. Neurons carry the messages of "hungry" or "sleepy" to your brain, and you respond appropriately.

All of our nerve cells have special fibers called **dendrites** and **axons.** Dendrites carry messages toward the cell body. Axons relay the messages away from the cell. The space between the axon of one nerve and the dendrite of a neighboring nerve is called a **synapse.** In order for nerve signals to travel through the nervous system, they must cross one synapse after another. This is where neurotransmitters come in. These are chemicals that carry the message or signal across the space between nerve cells. In some ways, they are like ferry boats. The passengers they carry are all the sensations we experience at any given time.

Most doctors and research scientists agree that ADHD is, in part, a result of chemical imbalances in the brain. Because of their particular genetic make up, children with ADHD have brains that make and use neurotransmitters differently from children who do not have ADHD. As a result, certain messages are blocked. There may not be enough of a certain neurotransmitter to carry the message from neuron to neuron. This might explain, for example, why children with ADHD have trouble focusing. Messages telling them to pay attention

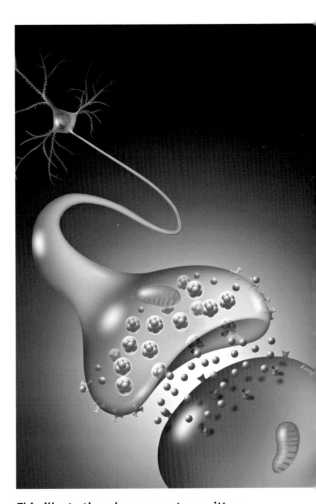

This illustration shows neurotransmitters (the round pink balls) traveling across the synapse from the axon of one cell to the dendrite of another.

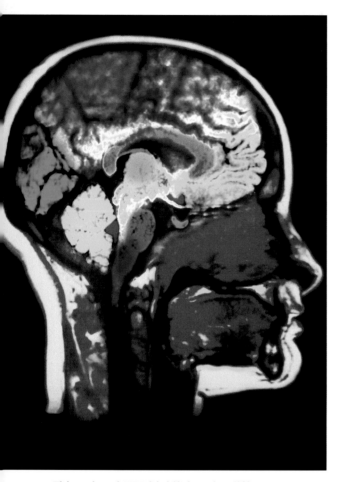

This colored MRI highlights the different parts of the brain. Problems with specific parts of a person's brain help doctors identify illness or injuries.

simply are not reaching their destination.

Scientists have pinpointed a number of neurotransmitters involved with ADHD. **Dopamine** helps nerve cells communicate with each other. **Norepinephrine** is involved with concentration and paying attention, especially during an emergency. Serotonin affects sleep and mood. Someone who does not have enough serotonin may feel depressed or have sleep problems. Gaba instructs other neurons to stop sending messages. When this happens, the person can begin to relax.

Since the 1990s, researchers studying ADHD have been able to see deeply into the living human brain using advanced techniques, such as magnetic resonance imaging (MRI). They can now compare the brains of children with ADHD against the brains of children who do not have ADHD. The images reveal some startling differences.

For one thing, ADHD brains tend to have a smaller prefrontal cortex. This part of the brain filters incoming information and helps a person figure out what to pay attention to and what to ignore. With a smaller prefrontal cortex, children with ADHD can become overwhelmed with incoming data. Instead of being able to separate important from unimportant information, they perceive everything as equally important and needing attention. For a student sitting in a classroom, this might mean his teacher's explanation of fractions is just as worthy of his attention as the sounds outside the classroom. No matter how hard he tries, he just cannot shut out the other sounds and focus on the math lesson.

The prefrontal cortex is one

Until recently, scientists thought the only kind of exchange between brain cells was chemical. They knew that neurotransmitters passed from the axon of one neuron to the dendrites of the next neuron. But current research has shown that in addition to chemicals, nerves also transmit electrical signals, or impulses.

These electrical signals are tracked by an electroencephalogram (EEG). During an EEG, a technician attaches pads to the patient's head. Wires from the pads are connected to a machine. This machine measures the amount of electricity a person's brain is transmitting when neurons are sending out electrical impulses.

Research may soon show that people with ADHD have unique or different EEG results. One day it may be possible to test for ADHD simply by using an EEG.

of four regions of the brain that have to do with memory. The other three are the hippocampus, amygdala, and corpus callosum. All four structures are smaller in the brains of children with ADHD. As a result, these children are more forgetful. Their long-term memory functions without any problem, so they can remember what happened to them in the past. But when it comes to daily homework assignments or household chores, their short-term memory fails them. It is not their fault. They forget these things because their brains are differently designed.

DIAGNOSING ADHD

The sooner a child receives a diagnosis, the better it will be for the child and for his or her family. Parents can begin a course of treatment once they know their child has ADHD. This may help the child avoid the secondary effects of ADHD, such as low self-esteem and lack of confidence in his or her abilities. But only a qualified professional can make an ADHD diagnosis. It is often very hard to tell the difference between normally active children and children with ADHD. Also, a professional must be able to separate out other issues that might be causing problems for the child. These include such things as emotional or psychological problems, family problems, or physical disabilities.

By themselves, none of the symptoms of ADHD are

Through various activities, tests, and conversations, a doctor may determine whether or not a child has ADHD.

out-of-the-ordinary, or abnormal. Most young children are easily distracted, love to talk, and enjoy physical activity. But when the symptoms are long-lasting and severe, it may be time to seek professional counseling.

The American Academy of Pediatrics has devised a set of guidelines for qualified professionals to use when making a diagnosis. These guidelines apply to school-age children between six and twelve years of age. Two of the guidelines include

• A child who shows signs of inattention, hyperactivity, impulsivity, or poor school performance should be evaluated for ADHD.

- In order to be diagnosed with ADHD, a child must meet the criteria for ADHD in the *DSM (Diagnostic and Statistical Manual of Mental Disorders)*.

The *DSM* states that a child being evaluated for ADHD must show at least two of the core symptoms. In addition, the symptoms must be long-lasting and intense. To make a diagnosis, the doctor has to gather evidence of how the symptoms express themselves in different settings, such as at home or in school. Where does this evidence come from? It comes from interviews with parents or caregivers as well as with a teacher or other school professional. It also comes from interviews with the child. What is most important is the child's personal history. Through interviews and observations, the doctor tries to see how the child is getting along at home, in school, and with friends and siblings. What problems might be occurring? Are these problems the result of family issues or can they be traced to ADHD once other causes are ruled out? Sometimes doctors will use psychological tests to help them make a diagnosis. But for the most part, they will rely on these in-depth interviews.

Once the official diagnosis is made, a course of treatment is decided. This treatment—often a combination of medication and therapy—will help the child handle everyday life.

Who Can Diagnose ADHD?

Type of specialist	Can diagnose ADHD	Can prescribe medication, if needed	Provides counseling or training
Psychiatrist	Yes	Yes	Yes
Psychologist	Yes	No	Yes
Pediatrician or Family Doctor	Yes	Yes	No
Social Worker	Yes	No	Yes

Adapted from a brochure from the National Institute of Mental Health (NIMH)

Psychiatrist: A medical doctor who specializes in how the mind works and in helping patients understand the causes of their emotional or mental problems. This kind of physician can diagnose ADHD and also prescribe medication.

Psychologist: A professional counselor with a graduate degree in psychology. Psychologists can provide individual or group therapy and diagnose ADHD. They cannot prescribe medication because they have not attended medical school.

Social Worker: A professional with an undergraduate degree in social work and possibly advanced degrees. Social workers help people who have problems like getting along with others. They usually have some sort of specialty like working with older people, teenagers who have committed crimes, or children with family problems.

3

THE HISTORY OF ADD AND ADHD

The medical condition known as Attention Deficit Hyperactivity Disorder has probably been around since the beginning of civilization. Over 2,500 years ago, the ancient Greek physician Hippocrates described a condition that resembles the symptoms of ADHD. He noted that his patients had "quickened responses to sensory experience, but also less tenaciousness [persistence] because the soul moves on quickly to the next impression." Hippocrates blamed this condition on an "overbalance of fire over water." He prescribed "barley rather than wheat bread, fish rather than meat, water drinks, and many natural and diverse physical activities."

PARENTAL INFLUENCE?

Another early description of what it is like to have ADHD appeared in an 1845 poem by Heinrich Hoffman, a German doctor. The title of the poem in English is *Fidgety Phil.* In this poem, Phil is constantly on the go. He is full of energy, and nothing will stop him. In modern terms, Phil is hyperactive. But in 1845, when the poem was written, people blamed Phil's wild behavior on his parents. They thought if his parents had exercised more discipline, Phil and children like him would have more self-control.

It was not until the early twentieth century that modern scientists and doctors began to seriously study the symptoms associated with this condition. Were the symptoms the result of how a child had been raised, or were they due to other causes, such as brain damage, disease, or environmental poisons?

BRAIN DAMAGE?

In 1902 a British pediatrician, George Frederick Still, gave a series of lectures at the Royal College of Physicians in Great Britain. During these lectures, he

Fidgety Phillip

Written by Heinrich Hoffmann in 1845, the poem is one of the earliest known descriptions of how a child with ADHD behaves. Here are a few verses of the poem:

*Let me see if Philip can
Be a little gentleman
Let me see, if he is able
To sit still for once at table:
Thus Papa bade Phil behave;
And Mamma look'd very grave.
But fidgety Phil, He won't sit still;
He wriggles and giggles,
And then, I declare
Swings backwards and forwards
And tilts up his chair,
Just like any rocking horse;
"Philip! I am getting cross!"*

*See the naughty restless child
Growing still more rude and wild.
Till his chair falls over quite.
Philip screams with all his might.
Catches at the cloth, but then
That makes matters worse again.
Down upon the ground they fall.
Glasses, plates, knives, forks and all.
How Mamma did fret and frown.
When she saw them tumbling down!
And Papa made such a face!
Philip is in sad disgrace.*

described a group of children he had treated. They each had trouble controlling themselves and tended to do whatever they felt like doing. When authority figures like parents or teachers tried to stop them, these children often became rebellious. In Dr. Still's words, they were lacking "inhibitory volition" and were "passionate and defiant."

Unlike Heinrich Hoffman, Dr. Still believed unruly, overactive children act that way not because of their parents, but because of some problem with their brains. He was one of the first medical researchers to argue that the behavior of such children has biological causes. He believed that there was something in their physical make up that was responsible for their lack of control. But in the early part of the twentieth century, scientists were very far from understanding what that "something" was. Much more research and study would still need to be done.

After World War I, which lasted from 1914 to 1918, two things happened that reinforced Dr. Still's point of view. First, many soldiers who had fought in Europe came home with severe head injuries. Secondly, there was an outbreak of a deadly disease known as encephalitis. This virus was caused by mosquitoes. When a person was bitten by a mosquito that carried the virus, the person developed encephalitis. This illness affects the brain and can cause death. Both the injured soldiers and the patients with encephalitis were showing similar symptoms. They were overactive and had trouble controlling their impulses and staying focused. Their behavior clearly had nothing to do with how their parents had raised them. The behaviors seemed directly related to physical causes, like injury or disease. The condition came to be known as Post-Encephalitic Behavior Disorder. In 1934 a similar condition was named Organic Drivenness.

In 1937, Dr. Charles Bradley, a pediatrician at the Emma Bradley Hospital in Rhode Island, was treating children with similar sorts of behaviors. They had trouble concentrating, could not sit still at

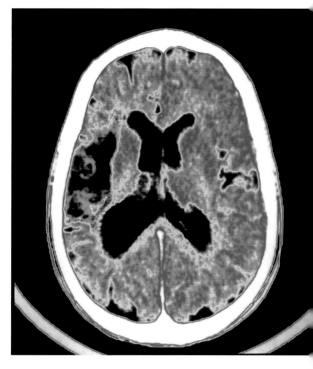

This scan—called a CT or CAT scan— shows the brain of a child with encephalitis. Encephalitis makes part of the brain swell (shown on the left in black and green) and can cause brain damage.

school, and acted on impulse without thinking too much about the consequences. Dr. Bradley prescribed a drug called Benzedrine. The drug had a very positive effect. The children called their medication "arithmetic pills" because it helped them sit still long enough to do their math lessons.

The next major advance in the study of ADHD came in the 1940s when the United States was at war with Germany and

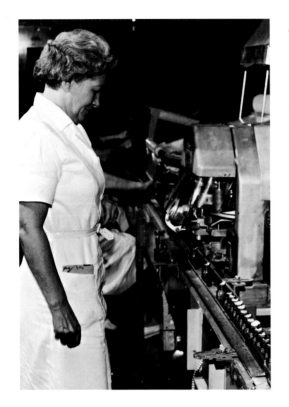

A worker watches as Ritalin tablets are packaged at a factory in the 1960s.

Japan. Like soldiers who had fought in World War I, American soldiers returning home with head injuries during World War II were overactive and had short attention spans. Researchers and doctors concluded that these symptoms must be linked to the brain. They believed that some form of brain damage, which could have happened at birth or through injury or disease, caused uncontrollable behavior in children or adults. Instead of Organic Drivenness, the syndrome became known as Minimal Brain Dysfunction.

In 1956 doctors for the first time began prescribing the drug Ritalin for the treatment of ADHD. But despite the drug's effectiveness, researchers still questioned if brain damage alone was the leading cause.

HYPERACTIVE CHILDREN

In 1960 Dr. Stella Chess, a highly respected child psychiatrist, began to study hyperactivity. Her research convinced her that this symptom could appear in children who had no brain damage whatsoever. If that was the case, then how could doctors explain why some children were so overactive? Dr. Chess and other researchers used the term "hyperactive child syndrome" to characterize these children. They believed the childrens' symptoms had nothing to do with the home environment or with brain damage. According to their research, hyperactive children behaved the way they did because of their unique biology.

However, not everyone agreed with them. In the 1950s and 1960s, more and more children began showing signs of ADHD. Many of these children had no history of head injury, brain damage, or disease. Researchers concluded that poor parenting must have caused their ADHD symptoms. If the parents could learn better child-raising skills, then perhaps their children's behavior would improve.

Through the 1960s and 1970s, many scientists studied hyperactivity in children. One of the most influential of these scientists was a Canadian psychologist named Virginia Douglas. She identified several major characteristics of the syndrome that was then called Hyperkinetic Reaction of Childhood.

Short attention span and poor control of impulses were two of the leading characteristics. In 1980, as a result of her work, the American Psychiatric Association renamed the syndrome Attention Deficit Disorder with or without Hyperactivity. The new name appeared for the first time in the third edition of the *Diagnostic and Statistical Manual,* or *DSM III.* Doctors use this handbook to determine if a person has a mental disorder. In this manual, a person with ADD had to suffer from inattention, hyperactivity, and poor impulse control. Scientists and doctors were finally recognizing ADD as a medical condition that could be diagnosed and treated.

But the naming and renaming did not stop there. In 1987 the *DSM III* was revised. In the revised edition of this manual, ADD was changed to ADHD or Attention Deficit Hyperactivity Disorder. But the name change was at first confusing to many people. The new name implied that in order for a child to be diagnosed he or she had to be hyperactive. But hyperactivity is only one of the symptoms of ADHD. And many children who have this condition are not necessarily hyperactive.

In 1994 the American Psychiatric Association tried to clear up this confusion. The fourth edition of the *DSM* described three distinct types of ADHD, depending on which symptom was most outstanding. *DSM IV* also stated that in order for there to be a diagnosis of ADHD, the child must start showing symptoms before age seven and in two or more situations, such as home and school. The tree types of ADHD are

- ADHD-I–ADHD primarily inattentive, no hyperactivity
- ADHD–HI–ADHD primarily hyperactive-impulsive
- ADHD–C–ADHD combined inattention and hyperactivity

In the past, the medication used to treat ADHD worked quickly and lasted for about four hours. But in 2000, the U.S. Food and Drug Administration (FDA) approved the first slow-release ADHD medication. This new version could be given once a day and lasted twelve hours. One year later, the

Advances in technology have helped experts diagnose and treat attention disorders like ADHD. Some learning centers use special computer programs to help a child with ADHD focus and control impulses.

American Academy of Pediatrics published a set of general recommendations for treating children with ADHD. Later that year, the American Academy of Child and Adolescent Psychiatry published guidelines for treating ADHD symptoms with specific drugs called stimulants. In 2002, the FDA approved the first non-stimulant medication for ADHD.

New treatments continue to be researched and developed. As technology improves, and our understanding of the brain and chemical imbalances progresses, methods of treatment will be more efficient. This will be good news for anybody with ADHD.

4

LIVING WITH THE DISORDER

ADHD affects just about every area of a child's life. Relationships with parents or caregivers, siblings (brothers and sisters), friends, classmates, and teachers all reflect difficulties with impulse control, hyperactivity, and inattention. At school, a child with ADHD is likely to have trouble keeping up with lessons, completing assignments, and turning in projects on time. Low grades and underachievement are likely to lower self-esteem and weaken self-confidence.

At home, the child may also have problems. It is not uncommon for a child with ADHD to feel jealous of siblings who do not have ADHD when they receive more praise for "being good." On the other hand, brothers and sisters might resent the fact that their sibling with ADHD is getting more attention because he or she needs it. And parents or caregivers might feel frustrated, disappointed, and angry if all their efforts to help their child seem to be failing.

Some children with ADHD do not make friends easily or tend to lose the friends they do have when their symptoms get in the way. A child who has temper tantrums when he or she does not get his or her own way may face rejection by other children. If the child does not follow directions well or becomes easily distracted during a game or other group activity, he or she might be put on the sidelines much of the time.

To help a child with ADHD feel confident and competent in all the important parts of his or her life, some form of treatment is necessary. Many professional childcare workers recommend a team approach to treatment. The team is typically made up of the child's parents, teacher, and doctor

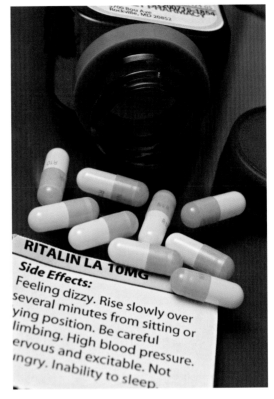

Ritalin is the most popular drug used to treat symptoms of ADHD.

all working together and supporting each other. Other team members might include the school guidance counselor or social worker, resource professionals like a reading specialist, and possibly an outside psychotherapist or psychologist.

While there are many strategies for managing and treating ADHD, what seems to work best is a combination of medication, counseling, help in school, and a well-structured home environment.

MEDICATION

Symptoms or problems related to having ADHD can usually be grouped into two categories: primary and secondary. The primary, or core problems, are the actual symptoms of ADHD— hyperactivity, inattention, and impulsivity. Most experts believe the only effective treatment for these symptoms is medication, which only a doctor can prescribe.

There are two basic types of medication that doctors use to treat ADHD. The most widely used are stimulant drugs like Ritalin and Dexedrine. Both of these drugs affect the central nervous system (the brain, the spine, and the nerves) by making more neurotransmitters available for use. Scientists still do not know exactly how this happens or in which parts of the brain these chemicals are made. But what they do know for sure is that stimulant drugs boost the production of dopamine and norepinephrine. These two neurotransmitters help reduce ADHD symptoms.

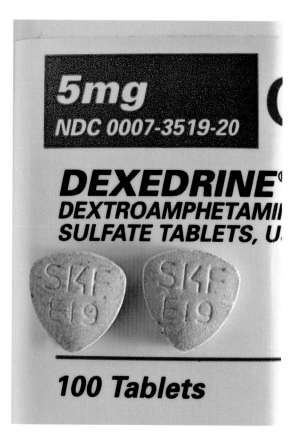

Dexedrine is usually taken in pill form.

Dopamine plays an important role in increasing attentiveness and awareness of a person's surroundings. Norepinephrine helps someone become more alert to signs of danger or problems in that person's environment. By creating the right balance of these and other neurotransmitters, stimulant drugs like Ritalin or Dexedrine have many positive benefits for children with ADHD. These medications reduce mood swings and irritability. They improve concentration and can help the child focus better. They also help the child feel more in control of his or her impulses, and reduce feelings of frustration and **anxiety.**

Of course, there is no "magic pill" that will take away all the symptoms of ADHD. The doctor may need to experiment with a combination of drugs until the right ones are found. The doctor may also need to gradually increase or decrease the dosage before the child begins to respond in a positive way. Too little of a medication may have no effect at all. On the other hand, too big a dose may cause unpleasant side effects like dry mouth or trouble sleeping. Once the doctor finds the right combination of drugs, and the right dosage, then the child can expect improvement in about a week or so. Some stimulants only last a few hours, so the medication must be taken several times each day. Other stimulants have longer-lasting effects, and can be taken less often.

Studies show that for about 85 percent of children with ADHD, stimulant drugs do work. But for those children who do not experience any improvement in their symptoms, doctors can try administering another type of medication called **antidepressants.** These drugs are mainly used to treat depression and anxiety in people who do not have ADHD. However, they are also beneficial in the treatment of children with ADHD. The most commonly used antidepressants for ADHD are tricyclics like Norpramin.

Recently, doctors have begun prescribing other kinds of antidepressants. These newer drugs are called **SSRIs,** or Selective Serotonin Reuptake Inhibitors. Prozac and Zoloft are examples of SSRIs that can reduce ADHD symptoms. Both medications increase the amount of serotonin in the brain. Serotonin is a neurotransmitter that helps to regulate sleep, mood, and appetite. It is found in the brain and also in the digestive tract.

In addition to stimulant drugs and antidepressants, a third kind of drug is also available for treating ADHD. It works by creating a balance in the brain between two different neurotransmitters—norepinephrine and **epinephrine.** When the brain has just the right amounts of these chemicals, the person with ADHD may find the symptoms diminishing. Drugs in this third category are called **SNRIs,** or Selective Norepinephrine Reuptake Inhibitors. They are neither stimulants nor antidepressants.

When medication is effective, the child with ADHD can expect to feel calmer, more focused, and more in control. In

ADHD Medications and What They Do

Type of Drug	Class of Medicine	Effects
Ritalin	Stimulant	Balances release of dopamine. Helps control impulses. Improves attention.
Adderall	Stimulant	Balances release of dopamine. Helps control impulses. Improves attention.
Concerta	Stimulant	Balances release of dopamine. Helps control impulses. Sharpens attention.
Strattera	Non-stimulant; a type of SNRI (selective norepinephrine reuptake inhibitor)	Balances the release of two neurotransmitters: norepinephrine and epinephrine. Helps control impulses and improve attention.
Zoloft, Prozac	Antidepressants that are SSRIs (selective serotonin reuptake inhibitors)	Balances level of serotonin in the brain. The right level can relieve depression, improve sleep, and intensify the positive effects of ADHD medications.

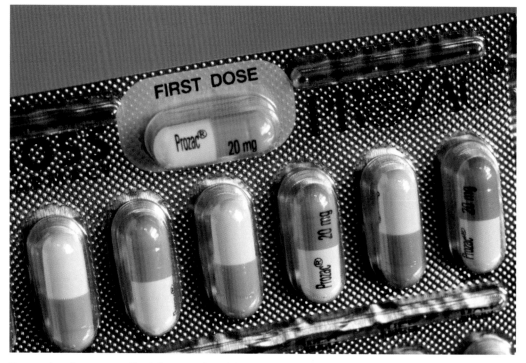

Prozac is often prescribed for people with ADHD, but it can also be used to treat emotional disorders.

time, as the symptoms improve, the child will hopefully gain a sense of well-being, feel more self-confident, and see himself or herself in a much more positive way.

HELP AT SCHOOL

In addition to home and community, school is one of the most important settings of a child's life. After all, it is where the child spends up to seven hours every day of the week. Children with ADHD often have learning disabilities in addition to their problems with concentration and focusing. They may do very well in one subject, but do poorly in others. Because of their ADHD, they may spend too much time doing their homework, forget to bring their assignments home, or forget to turn them in even when they have completed them. They may also get into trouble for talking too much in class, daydreaming, or getting out of their seats at inappropriate times. Without help, these children will fall behind in their studies.

For these reasons, it is very important that children with ADHD take part in special programs designed to improve their chances of success. One such program is called the 504 Plan. To set up this program, students first meet with their teachers, parents, and school counselor. The purpose of this planning

Other Treatments

Besides traditional medication, healthcare professionals have tried out other treatments that seem to help children with ADHD. One such treatment is biofeedback. In this form of treatment, a machine monitors a person's heart rate, breathing, and brain waves when he or she is calm and focused and when the person is anxious or having problems. Over the course of many sessions, the person watches the monitor, and tries to adjust how he or she feels until the brain waves on the monitor look like they do when he or she feels focused and calm.

Other kinds of treatment for ADHD include hypnosis, herbal remedies, taking large doses of vitamins, and going on a diet free of certain chemicals or ingredients called food additives. There is no scientific evidence that these alternative treatments are effective. In some cases, they may be dangerous to the health of the person with ADHD. A person with ADHD should always consult a healthcare professional before attempting any form of treatment.

Most schools are required by law to accommodate students who have learning disorders or similar problems in school. This is done so that all children are given equal opportunities to learn and succeed in school.

meeting is to decide what changes need to be made in the classroom. For instance, a student's 504 Plan may mean his or her desk will be closer to the front of the room so he or she can follow the teacher more closely. The teacher may give the student more time to take tests, give shorter homework assignments, or more class time to work on assignments. The teacher might also agree to change teaching methods in order to help the student with ADHD learn more easily.

The 504 Plans are part of a special anti-discrimination law. Under this law, any organization that accepts money from the

In many classrooms you may find students with ADHD working alongside their classmates.

federal government must assist people with disabilities. Since this law covers public schools, the schools must provide for any child diagnosed with ADHD.

Another learning plan is called the Individualized Education Program (IEP). These programs go further than 504 Plans in assisting children with ADHD. To qualify for enrollment, a child must be diagnosed and then take a comprehensive series of tests. These tests measure intelligence, evaluate learning disabilities, check general health, hearing, and vision, and explore any emotional problems the child might have.

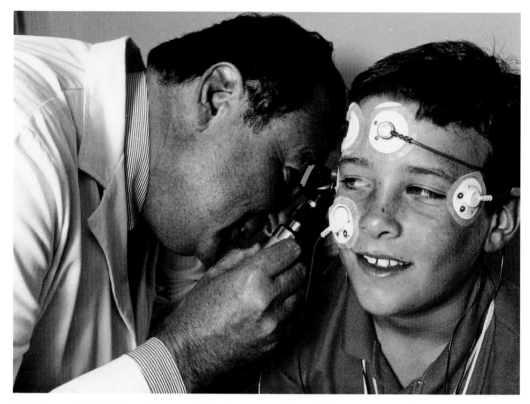

Children with ADHD need to see their doctors and specialists on a regular schedule. This will help everyone monitor the disorder and the progress of its treatments.

Schools are legally required to provide IEPs because of a federal law called Individuals with Disabilities Education Act (IDEA). This law states that every school-age child in the United States must receive free and appropriate public education. For children with ADHD, an appropriate education might mean one that includes special services. These can include speech therapy, occupational therapy, reading help, and counseling with the school psychologist or guidance counselor.

COUNSELING AND COACHING

Medication treats the actual symptoms of ADHD, such as short attention span or hyperactivity. But children with ADHD often develop feelings of low-esteem, anger, depression, and other emotional problems. They may also have trouble making or keeping friends or getting along with their parents. Counseling can help with these related, or secondary problems.

Counseling is basically an opportunity for a child to talk about the problems he or she is having at home, in school, or in other parts of life. A counselor is a trained professional

Counseling is helpful for treating a variety of health issues or disorders.

whose job is to listen, to offer advice, and to help the person find better ways of dealing with others and with handling his problems. A counselor also tries to create a safe environment in which the person can express feelings without fear of judgment or ridicule. A counselor can be a psychologist, psychotherapist, social worker, or psychiatrist.

The parents of a child with ADHD can arrange to have private sessions with a counselor. An alternative form of counseling is group therapy. In group therapy, the counselor sees several children at the same time. Problems caused by ADHD are more likely to come up during group therapy. In individual counseling, on the other hand, it might be easier for the child with ADHD to sit still and stay focused.

Older students with ADHD sometimes form support groups. A trained professional might lead the group. But this does not have to be the case. The members of the group may just want to get together and talk about their problems and concerns, and share whatever they have learned about managing their disorder better.

Coaching has become a very popular way for people with ADHD to get the help and support they need. A coach can be a social worker, college student, teacher, or friend. In this form of counseling, the coach acts much the way a sports coach does. The coach encourages the children with ADHD to do their best and not give up no matter how tough it gets. But unlike a football or baseball coach, a coach working with someone with

One-on-one help from a teacher or a learning specialist helps many students with ADHD.

ADHD helps that person organize his or her life. For example, say a student with ADHD has a big science project due in a few weeks. The personal coach might help the student figure out what has to be done in order to complete the project. Together they will decide on an order or sequence of steps. For instance, first they will go to the library and find at least three books on the topic being studied. The following steps could include deciding what other materials they will need, when they will put it all together, and how they will balance their time so that the project is done by the due date.

If the student is having trouble focusing, the coach is there to remind the student of the next step that he or she needs to take. The coach can help in person, on the phone, or even by email. The main thing is for the coach to help the student create some kind of structure so that the student will not feel completely disorganized or overwhelmed. An effective coach will help children with ADHD do what they have trouble doing on their own. This could be paying attention, completing a task, or deciding what needs to be done now and what can wait.

HELP AT HOME

A child's most important relationships are with family members. The way parents raise their children will not cause or eliminate the symptoms of ADHD. But what the home environment is like will greatly affect how these children do in other parts of their lives. Like all children, children with ADHD need love and understanding. But they also need a well-structured home environment. To create such an environment, parents need to devote a great deal of planning and effort.

At home, children perform a number of daily activities like brushing their teeth, washing up, doing chores and homework, playing with siblings, and watching television. Children with ADHD may have problems keeping their room clean, getting ready for school, or completing assigned tasks. Whatever their problems at home, they need to take responsibility for their actions and not use ADHD as an excuse for bad behavior.

Parents can encourage their child to become responsible for himself or herself. They can also help their child learn how to manage the symptoms. One way to achieve these goals is through discipline. This means setting up rules that are firm, consistent, clear, and predictable. Firm means that following the rules always has the same rewards, while breaking them has the same punishments. Consistent means the rules stay the same from one day to the next. Clear means there is no question about what the rules mean. Predictable means the rules are made before misbehavior happens, not after. So the child with ADHD knows, for example, that homework must be completed before watching television.

Household rules apply only to the child's actions. They do not apply to the child's thoughts and feelings, and they are not intended to curb natural creativity. For children up to ages ten or eleven, parents need to be very clear about which behaviors need to be limited or changed. For example, they might tell their child that temper tantrums at bedtime are not okay. Parents also need to let their child know that some rules are more important than others. The consequences for following or breaking a particular rule will depend on the importance of that rule. If the family decides that brushing teeth before bedtime is a minor rule, for instance, then the consequence of forgetting will also be minor.

Children with ADHD need to know beforehand what they can

expect in the way of rewards and punishments. Rewards can be as simple as giving the child more attention or praise, a special privilege like staying up late on a weekend night, or even a small toy on occasion. Punishments should not involve any kind of abuse. Instead, they should be limited to sending the child to a time-out space or to his or her room until the child regains control.

In addition to discipline, another useful strategy for creating a structured home environment is a symptoms management plan or a behavior management plan. The purpose of the plan is to help the child better manage his symptoms at home and in other settings. The plan works best if the child takes part in creating it. First, parents help their child identify his or her own particular symptoms. Working together, the family tries to come up with coping or managing tactics that fit

Many teachers and learning specialists believe that time-outs can help children with ADHD understand how to control their impulses.

each symptom. For example, a child with inattention problems frequently forgets to do his homework or complete his chores. For the problem with homework, a possible coping tactic might be a written schedule. Each night the child writes out what assignments are due the following day. They are checked off the list as they are completed. For chores, the child might follow a set of written instructions that explain what needs to be done. For example, if one of the chores is to clean his room at least once a week, then the instructions will spell out what that means: put dirty clothes in a laundry basket; hang up clean clothes; put away toys; clean under the bed. Again, the child can check off each task as it is completed.

Every student has his or her way of dealing with homework and other school activities. Children with ADHD usually need more help structuring their time.

ADHD and Aging

....

ADHD can affect people of all ages. In the past, experts thought that only children could have ADHD, and that they would eventually outgrow it. But most experts today do not agree with that theory. Many children with ADHD do not outgrow the disorder. In most cases, they continue to take medication and practice coping tactics for many years. Additionally, coping techniques and symptom management often become easier when the person has been handling the disorder for many years. When they manage their disorder properly, children with ADHD can grow to become adults with fulfilling lives. Adults with ADHD work in professional jobs, have families, and can have fun-filled lives.

Recent studies have shown that there are many adults living with ADHD who might not be aware of it, or who only discovered it later in life. This is most likely because they were not diagnosed with the disorder when they were younger. Some symptoms of ADHD in adults include difficulty with organization, taking on many projects and not being able to finish any of them, trouble focusing on the task at hand, becoming distracted easily, and acting or saying whatever he or she feels without considering the consequences. Medication, counseling, and other professional help can help adults with ADHD cope with the disorder. But adults who think they might have ADHD should always talk to their doctor first. A doctor can rule out other illnesses that may be causing the symptoms.

For other ADHD symptoms like hyperactivity or poor impulse control, parents and children can use the same basic method— identify the symptoms and where they are most likely to occur, and then come up with coping tactics for each one. Effective symptoms management will not happen overnight. It may take a good deal of trial-and-error for parents and children to find a set of tactics that work. Ideally, these tactics should build on the

With careful diagnosis, a well-thought-out treatment plan, and a lot of patience and understanding, children with ADHD can lead productive and happy lives.

child's strengths. As the child learns to manage the symptoms, he or she will feel more in charge of his or her own life.

For children, having ADHD can be a very frustrating experience. But with a strong support system, proper treatment, and a caring, structured home environment, the child with ADHD stands an excellent chance of becoming a successful, productive adult. Many successful and talented people have ADHD. Their symptoms did not stand in their way of achieving greatness. If anything, ADHD often goes hand-in-hand with many positive qualities like imagination, creativity, and an exceptional potential for growth.

GLOSSARY

antidepressants—A group of medications used to treat depression, anxiety, and ADHD.

anxiety—Feelings of fear or worry.

axons—Parts of a nerve cell that carry signals, or impulses away from the cell.

dendrites—Long, thin nerve fibers that receive signals from other nerve cells and pass them along to the cell body.

diagnose—To determine what is causing health or behavioral problems.

dopamine—A naturally-formed brain chemical that helps the nerves do their job.

epinephrine—A substance produced in the adrenal glands (which are above the kidneys) that increases heart rate and blood pressure; also called adrenaline.

hyperactivity—An unusually high amount of activity and energy.

hyperfocus—The ability to concentrate on a topic or activity and almost entirely shut out unwanted distractions.

impulsivity—Acting on impulse often without thinking about the consequences or planning ahead.

neurons—A special name for nerve cells, which make up the brain, nerves, and spinal cord, and which send and receive signals to and from the brain and nervous system.

neurotransmitters—Chemicals released by neurons that regulate the flow of electrical and chemical signals, or impulses from one nerve cell to the next.

norepinephrine—A substance very similar to epinephrine and produced in the adrenal glands to regulate heart rate and blood pressure.

psychiatrist—A medical doctor who diagnoses and treats mental illness.

Ritalin—The name of a stimulant medication used to treat ADHD.

self-esteem—How a person feels about himself or herself.

SNRIs (Selective Norepinephrine Reuptake Inhibitors)—A type of antidepressant medication that increases the level of Norepinephrine in the brain.

SSRIs (Selective Serotonin Reuptake Inhibitors)—A type of antidepressant medication that increases the level of serotonin in the brain.

synapse—The gap between the axon of one nerve cell and the dendrite of a neighboring nerve cell.

therapist—Professional healthcare worker who is trained to help people with their emotional or family problems.

FIND OUT MORE

Organizations

Attention Deficit Disorder Association (ADDA)
15000 Commerce Parkway, Suite C
Mount Laurel, NJ 08054
856-439-9099
http://www.add.org/contact/index.html

Attention Deficit Disorder Association, ADDA, is a leading ADD and ADHD organization. It provides information, resources and networking opportunities to help people with ADD or ADHD.

CHADD—Children and Adults with Attention Deficit Hyperactivity Disorder
8181 Professional Place - Suite 150
Landover, MD 20785
301-306-7070
http://www.chadd.org

CHADD is a national non-profit organization dedicated to helping individuals in ADHD and their families.

Books

Peacock, Judith. *ADD and ADHD.* Mankato, MN: LifeMatters, 2002.

Petersen, Christine. *Does Everyone Have ADHD: A Teen's Guide to Diagnosis and Treatment.* New York: Franklin Watts, 2006.

Pigach, Philippa. *ADHD.* Chicago: Heinemann Library, 2004.

Taylor, John F. *The Survival Guide for Kids with ADD or ADHD.* Minneapolis, MN: Free Spirit, 2006.

Walker, Beth. *The Girls' Guide to ADHD.* Bethesda, MD: Woodbine House, 2004.

Williams, Julie. *Attention-Deficit/Hyperactivity Disorder.* Berkeley Heights, NJ: Enslow Publishers, 2001.

Web Sites

ADDvance—Answers to Your Questions about ADD (ADHD)
http://www.ADDvance.com

ADHD—National Institute of Mental Health
http://www.nimh.nih.gov/HealthInformation/adhdmenu.cfm

Focus on ADHD
http://www.focusonadhd.com/faces/faces_child.jhtml

Kids' Heath: ADHD
http://www.kidshealth.org/teen/school_jobs/school/adhd.html

National Resource Center on ADHD
http://www.help4adhd.org/en/about/wwk

ABOUT THE AUTHOR

George Capaccio is both a writer and a storyteller. He loves to visit schools and perform stories from all over the world for young audiences. He also enjoys writing educational books about history and science. He lives in Arlington, Massachusetts, with his wife, Nancy, and their beautiful Golden Retriever.

INDEX

Page numbers for illustrations are in **boldface**